Day

A Book of Poems

D. H. Lawrence

Alpha Editions

This edition published in 2021

ISBN : 9789354595318

Design and Setting By
Alpha Editions
www.alphaedis.com
Email - info@alphaedis.com

As per information held with us this book is in Public Domain. This book is a reproduction of an important historical work. Alpha Editions uses the best technology to reproduce historical work in the same manner it was first published to preserve its original nature. Any marks or number seen are left intentionally to preserve its true form.

Contents

GUARDS!	- 1 -
EVOLUTIONS OF SOLDIERS	- 2 -
THE LITTLE TOWN AT EVENING	- 3 -
LAST HOURS	- 4 -
TOWN	- 5 -
AFTER THE OPERA	- 6 -
GOING BACK	- 7 -
ON THE MARCH	- 8 -
BOMBARDMENT	- 10 -
WINTER-LULL	- 11 -
THE ATTACK	- 12 -
OBSEQUIAL ODE	- 14 -
SHADES	- 16 -
BREAD UPON THE WATERS.	- 17 -
RUINATION	- 18 -
RONDEAU OF A CONSCIENTIOUS OBJECTOR.	- 19 -
	- 19 -
TOMMIES IN THE TRAIN	- 20 -
WAR-BABY	- 22 -

NOSTALGIA

GUARDS!

A Review in Hyde Park 1913.
The Crowd Watches.
WHERE the trees rise like cliffs, proud and
 blue-tinted in the distance,
Between the cliffs of the trees, on the grey-
 green park
Rests a still line of soldiers, red motionless range of
 guards
Smouldering with darkened busbies beneath the bay-
 onets' slant rain.

Colossal in nearness a blue police sits still on his horse
Guarding the path; his hand relaxed at his thigh,
And skyward his face is immobile, eyelids aslant
In tedium, and mouth relaxed as if smiling—ineffable
tedium!

So! So! Gaily a general canters across the space,
With white plumes blinking under the evening grey
 sky.
And suddenly, as if the ground moved
The red range heaves in slow, magnetic reply.

EVOLUTIONS OF SOLDIERS

The red range heaves and compulsory sways, ah see!
  in the flush of a march
Softly-impulsive advancing as water towards a weir
  from the arch
Of shadow emerging as blood emerges from inward
  shades of our night
Encroaching towards a crisis, a meeting, a spasm and
  throb of delight.

The wave of soldiers, the coming wave, the throbbing
  red breast of approach
Upon us; dark eyes as here beneath the busbies glit-
  tering, dark threats that broach
Our beached vessel; darkened rencontre inhuman, and
  closed warm lips, and dark
Mouth-hair of soldiers passing above us, over the wreck
  of our bark.

And so, it is ebb-time, they turn, the eyes beneath the
  busbies are gone.
But the blood has suspended its timbre, the heart from
  out of oblivion
Knows but the retreat of the burning shoulders, the
  red-swift waves of the sweet
Fire horizontal declining and ebbing, the twilit ebb of
  retreat.

THE LITTLE TOWN AT EVENING

THE chime of the bells, and the church clock
    striking eight
Solemnly and distinctly cries down the babel
    of children still playing in the hay.
The church draws nearer upon us, gentle and great
In shadow, covering us up with her grey.

Like drowsy children the houses fall asleep
Under the fleece of shadow, as in between
Tall and dark the church moves, anxious to keep
Their sleeping, cover them soft unseen.

Hardly a murmur comes from the sleeping brood,
I wish the church had covered me up with the rest
In the home-place. Why is it she should exclude
Me so distinctly from sleeping with those I love best?

LAST HOURS

THE cool of an oak's unchequered shade
    Falls on me as I lie in deep grass
    Which rushes upward, blade beyond blade,
    While higher the darting grass-flowers pass
    Piercing the blue with their crocketed spires
    And waving flags, and the ragged fires
    Of the sorrel's cresset—a green, brave town
    Vegetable, new in renown.

    Over the tree's edge, as over a mountain
    Surges the white of the moon,
    A cloud comes up like the surge of a fountain,
    Pressing round and low at first, but soon
    Heaving and piling a round white dome.
    How lovely it is to be at home
    Like an insect in the grass
    Letting life pass.

    There's a scent of clover crept through my hair
    From the full resource of some purple dome
    Where that lumbering bee, who can hardly bear
    His burden above me, never has clomb.
    But not even the scent of insouciant flowers
    Makes pause the hours.

    Down the valley roars a townward train.
    I hear it through the grass
    Dragging the links of my shortening chain
    Southwards, alas!

TOWN

LONDON
    Used to wear her lights splendidly,
    Flinging her shawl-fringe over the River,
    Tassels in abandon.

    And up in the sky
    A two-eyed clock, like an owl
    Solemnly used to approve, chime, chiming,
    Approval, goggle-eyed fowl.

    There are no gleams on the River,
    No goggling clock;
    No sound from St. Stephen's;
    No lamp-fringed frock.

    Instead,
    Darkness, and skin-wrapped
    Fleet, hurrying limbs,
    Soft-footed dead.

    London
    Original, wolf-wrapped
    In pelts of wolves, all her luminous
    Garments gone.

    London, with hair
    Like a forest darkness, like a marsh
    Of rushes, ere the Romans
    Broke in her lair.

    It is well
    That London, lair of sudden
    Male and female darknesses
    Has broken her spell.

AFTER THE OPERA

DOWN the stone stairs
  Girls with their large eyes wide with tragedy
  Lift looks of shocked and momentous emotion
   up at me.
  And I smile.

  Ladies
  Stepping like birds with their bright and pointed feet
  Peer anxiously forth, as if for a boat to carry them out
   of the wreckage,
  And among the wreck of the theatre crowd
  I stand and smile.

  They take tragedy so becomingly.
  Which pleases me.

  But when I meet the weary eyes
  The reddened aching eyes of the bar-man with thin
   arms,
  I am glad to go back to where I came from.

GOING BACK

THE NIGHT turns slowly round,
    Swift trains go by in a rush of light;
    Slow trains steal past.
    This train beats anxiously, outward bound.

    But I am not here.
    I am away, beyond the scope of this turning;
    There, where the pivot is, the axis
    Of all this gear.

    I, who sit in tears,
    I, whose heart is torn with parting;
    Who cannot bear to think back to the departure
      platform;
    My spirit hears

    Voices of men
    Sound of artillery, aeroplanes, presences,
    And more than all, the dead-sure silence,
    The pivot again.

    There, at the axis
    Pain, or love, or grief
    Sleep on speed; in dead certainty;
    Pure relief.

    There, at the pivot
    Time sleeps again.
    No has-been, no here-after; only the perfected
    Silence of men.

ON THE MARCH

WE are out on the open road.
  Through the low west window a cold light
    flows
  On the floor where never my numb feet trode
  Before; onward the strange road goes.

  Soon the spaces of the western sky
  With shutters of sombre cloud will close.
  But we'll still be together, this road and I,
  Together, wherever the long road goes.

  The wind chases by us, and over the corn
  Pale shadows flee from us as if from their foes.
  Like a snake we thresh on the long, forlorn
  Land, as onward the long road goes.

  From the sky, the low, tired moon fades out;
  Through the poplars the night-wind blows;
  Pale, sleepy phantoms are tossed about
  As the wind asks whither the wan road goes.

  Away in the distance wakes a lamp.
  Inscrutable small lights glitter in rows.
  But they come no nearer, and still we tramp
  Onward, wherever the strange road goes.

  Beat after beat falls sombre and dull.
  The wind is unchanging, not one of us knows
  What will be in the final lull
  When we find the place where this dead road goes.

  For something must come, since we pass and pass
  Along in the coiled, convulsive throes
  Of this marching, along with the invisible grass
  That goes wherever this old road goes.

  Perhaps we shall come to oblivion.

Perhaps we shall march till our tired toes
Tread over the edge of the pit, and we're gone
Down the endless slope where the last road goes.

If so, let us forge ahead, straight on
If we're going to sleep the sleep with those
That fall forever, knowing none
Of this land whereon the wrong road goes.

BOMBARDMENT

THE TOWN has opened to the sun.
    Like a flat red lily with a million petals
    She unfolds, she comes undone.

    A sharp sky brushes upon
    The myriad glittering chimney-tips
    As she gently exhales to the sun.

    Hurrying creatures run
    Down the labyrinth of the sinister flower.
    What is it they shun?

    A dark bird falls from the sun.
    It curves in a rush to the heart of the vast
    Flower: the day has begun.

WINTER-LULL

Because of the silent snow, we are all hushed
      Into awe.
No sound of guns, nor overhead no rushed
      Vibration to draw
Our attention out of the void wherein we are crushed.

A crow floats past on level wings
      Noiselessly.
Uninterrupted silence swings
      Invisibly, inaudibly
To and fro in our misgivings.

We do not look at each other, we hide
      Our daunted eyes.
White earth, and ruins, ourselves, and nothing beside.
      It all belies
Our existence; we wait, and are still denied.

We are folded together, men and the snowy ground
      Into nullity.
There is silence, only the silence, never a sound
      Nor a verity
To assist us; disastrously silence-bound!

THE ATTACK

WHEN we came out of the wood
   Was a great light!
   The night uprisen stood
   In white.

   I wondered, I looked around
   It was so fair. The bright
   Stubble upon the ground
   Shone white

   Like any field of snow;
   Yet warm the chase
   Of faint night-breaths did go
   Across my face!

   White-bodied and warm the night was,
   Sweet-scented to hold in my throat.
   White and alight the night was.
   A pale stroke smote

   The pulse through the whole bland being
   Which was This and me;
   A pulse that still went fleeing,
   Yet did not flee.

   After the terrible rage, the death,
   This wonder stood glistening?
   All shapes of wonder, with suspended breath,
   Arrested listening

   In ecstatic reverie.
   The whole, white Night!—
   With wonder, every black tree
   Blossomed outright.

   I saw the transfiguration
   And the present Host.

Transubstantiation
Of the Luminous Ghost.

OBSEQUIAL ODE

SURELY you've trodden straight
   To the very door!
   Surely you took your fate
Faultlessly. Now it's too late
   To say more.

     It is evident you were right,
       That man has a course to go
A voyage to sail beyond the charted seas.
You have passed from out of sight
     And my questions blow
Back from the straight horizon that ends all one sees.

     Now like a vessel in port
       You unlade your riches unto death,
And glad are the eager dead to receive you there.
     Let the dead sort
Your cargo out, breath from breath
Let them disencumber your bounty, let them all share.

     I imagine dead hands are brighter,
       Their fingers in sunset shine
With jewels of passion once broken through you as a
   prism
Breaks light into jewels; and dead breasts whiter
     For your wrath; and yes, I opine
They anoint their brows with your blood, as a perfect
   chrism.

     On your body, the beaten anvil,
       Was hammered out
That moon-like sword the ascendant dead unsheathe
Against us; sword that no man will
     Put to rout;
Sword that severs the question from us who breathe.

   Surely you've trodden straight

  To the very door.
You have surely achieved your fate;
And the perfect dead are elate
  To have won once more.

Now to the dead you are giving
  Your last allegiance.
But what of us who are living
And fearful yet of believing
  In your pitiless legions.

SHADES

SHALL I tell you, then, how it is?—
    There came a cloven gleam
    Like a tongue of darkened flame
    To flicker in me.

    And so I seem
    To have you still the same
    In one world with me.

    In the flicker of a flower,
    In a worm that is blind, yet strives,
    In a mouse that pauses to listen

    Glimmers our
    Shadow; yet it deprives
    Them none of their glisten.

    In every shaken morsel
    I see our shadow tremble
    As if it rippled from out of us hand in hand.

    As if it were part and parcel,
    One shadow, and we need not dissemble
    Our darkness: do you understand?

    For I have told you plainly how it is.

BREAD UPON THE WATERS.

SO you are lost to me!
    Ah you, you ear of corn straight lying,
    What food is this for the darkly flying
    Fowls of the Afterwards!

    White bread afloat on the waters,
    Cast out by the hand that scatters
    Food untowards,

    Will you come back when the tide turns?
    After many days? My heart yearns
    To know.

    Will you return after many days
    To say your say as a traveller says,
    More marvel than woe?

    Drift then, for the sightless birds
    And the fish in shadow-waved herds
    To approach you.

    Drift then, bread cast out;
    Drift, lest I fall in doubt,
    And reproach you.

    For you are lost to me!

RUINATION

THE sun is bleeding its fires upon the mist
    That huddles in grey heaps coiling and holding
      back.
    Like cliffs abutting in shadow a drear grey sea
    Some street-ends thrust forward their stack.

    On the misty waste-lands, away from the flushing grey
    Of the morning the elms are loftily dimmed, and tall
    As if moving in air towards us, tall angels
    Of darkness advancing steadily over us all.

RONDEAU OF A CONSCIENTIOUS

OBJECTOR.

THE hours have tumbled their leaden, mono-
   tonous sands
  And piled them up in a dull grey heap in the
   West.
  I carry my patience sullenly through the waste lands;
  To-morrow will pour them all back, the dull hours I
   detest.

I force my cart through the sodden filth that is pressed
Into ooze, and the sombre dirt spouts up at my hands
As I make my way in twilight now to rest.
The hours have tumbled their leaden, monotonous
  sands.

A twisted thorn-tree still in the evening stands
Defending the memory of leaves and the happy round
  nest.
But mud has flooded the homes of these weary lands
And piled them up in a dull grey heap in the West.

All day has the clank of iron on iron distressed
The nerve-bare place. Now a little silence expands
And a gasp of relief. But the soul is still compressed:
I carry my patience sullenly through the waste lands.

The hours have ceased to fall, and a star commands
Shadows to cover our stricken manhood, and blest
Sleep to make us forget: but he understands:
To-morrow will pour them all back, the dull hours
  I detest.

TOMMIES IN THE TRAIN

THE SUN SHINES,
    The coltsfoot flowers along the railway banks
    Shine like flat coin which Jove in thanks
    Strews each side the lines.

    A steeple
    In purple elms, daffodils
    Sparkle beneath; luminous hills
    Beyond—and no people.

    England, Oh Danaë
    To this spring of cosmic gold
    That falls on your lap of mould!
    What then are we?

What are we
Clay-coloured, who roll in fatigue
As the train falls league by league
From our destiny?

A hand is over my face,
A cold hand. I peep between the fingers
To watch the world that lingers
Behind, yet keeps pace.

Always there, as I peep
Between the fingers that cover my face!
Which then is it that falls from its place
And rolls down the steep?

Is it the train
That falls like meteorite
Backward into space, to alight
Never again?

Or is it the illusory world
That falls from reality

As we look? Or are we
Like a thunderbolt hurled?

One or another
Is lost, since we fall apart
Endlessly, in one motion depart
From each other.

WAR-BABY

THE CHILD like mustard-seed
   Rolls out of the husk of death
      Into the woman's fertile, fathomless lap.

Look, it has taken root!
See how it flourisheth.
   See how it rises with magical, rosy sap!

As for our faith, it was there
When we did not know, did not care;
   It fell from our husk like a little, hasty seed.

Sing, it is all we need.
Sing, for the little weed
   Will flourish its branches in heaven when we
     slumber beneath.

NOSTALGIA

THE WANING MOON looks upward; this
    grey night
  Slopes round the heavens in one smooth curve
  Of easy sailing; odd red wicks serve
To show where the ships at sea move out of sight.

The place is palpable me, for here I was born
Of this self-same darkness. Yet the shadowy house
    below
Is out of bounds, and only the old ghosts know
I have come, I feel them whimper in welcome, and
    mourn.

My father suddenly died in the harvesting corn
And the place is no longer ours. Watching, I hear
No sound from the strangers, the place is dark, and fear
Opens my eyes till the roots of my vision seems torn.

Can I go no nearer, never towards the door?
The ghosts and I we mourn together, and shrink
In the shadow of the cart-shed. Must we hover on
    the brink
Forever, and never enter the homestead any more?

Is it irrevocable? Can I really not go
Through the open yard-way? Can I not go past the
    sheds
And through to the mowie?—Only the dead in their
    beds
Can know the fearful anguish that this is so.

I kiss the stones, I kiss the moss on the wall,
And wish I could pass impregnate into the place.
I wish I could take it all in a last embrace.
I wish with my breast I here could annihilate it all.